SO-BZX-049

STATES

NEW MEXICO

A MyReportLinks.com Book

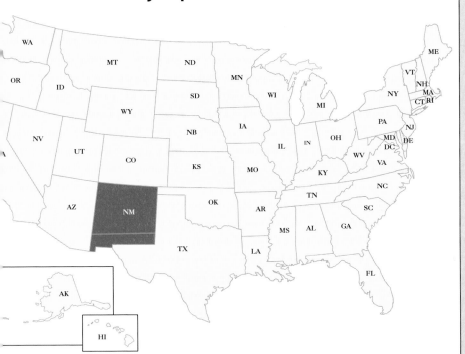

Judy Alter

MyReportLinks.com Books

an imprint of

 Enslow Publishers, Inc.

Box 398, 40 Industrial Road
Berkeley Heights, NJ 07922
USA

MyReportLinks.com Books, an imprint of Enslow Publishers, Inc.

Copyright © 2002 by Enslow Publishers, Inc.

All rights reserved.

No part of this book may be reproduced by any means
without the written permission of the publisher.

Library of Congress Cataloging-in-Publication Data

Alter, Judy, 1938–
   New Mexico / Judy Alter.
      p. cm.—(States)
   Summary: Discusses the land and climate, economy, government, and
history of New Mexico. Includes Internet links to Web sites.
   Includes bibliographical references and index.
   ISBN 0-7660-5098-X
   1. New Mexico—Juvenile literature. [1. New Mexico.] I. Title.
II. Series: States (Series : Berkeley Heights, N.J.)
F796.3.A48 2002
978.9—dc21

                                   2001008188

Printed in the United States of America

10 9 8 7 6 5 4 3 2 1

To Our Readers:
Through the purchase of this book, you and your library gain access to the Report Links that specifically back up this book.
The Publisher will provide access to the Report Links that back up this book and will keep these Report Links up to date on **www.myreportlinks.com** for three years from the book's first publication date.
We have done our best to make sure all Internet addresses in this book were active and appropriate when we went to press. However, the author and the Publisher have no control over, and assume no liability for, the material available on those Internet sites or on other Web sites they may link to.
The usage of the MyReportLinks.com Books Web site is subject to the terms and conditions stated on the Usage Policy Statement on **www.myreportlinks.com**.
In the future, a password may be required to access the Report Links that back up this book. The password is found on the bottom of page 4 of this book.

Photo Credits: © Corel Corporation, pp. 3, 10, 14, 16, 19, 21; © PhotoDisc, Inc., p.22; Courtesy of America's Story from America's Library/Library of Congress, pp. 12, 24, 42; Courtesy of Georgia O'Keeffe Museum, p. 18; Courtesy of MyReportLinks.com Books, p. 4; Courtesy of New Mexico: Land of Enchantment, p. 20; Courtesy of Cultures.com, p. 22; Courtesy of The National Atomic Museum, p. 26; Courtesy of Governor Johnson's Home Page, p. 29; Courtesy of New Mexico Museum of Natural History & Science, p. 34; Courtesy of New Mexico.org, p. 31; Courtesy of PBS: New Perspectives on the West, pp. 35, 40; Courtesy of XII Travelers: Memorial of the Southwest, p. 36; Enslow Publishers, Inc., pp. 1, 38; Library of Congress, p. 3 (Constitution).

Cover Photo: © 1998 Corbis Corporation
Cover Description: Chaco Canyon, New Mexico.

Contents

MyReportLinks.com Books
Great Books, Great Links, Great for Research!

MyReportLinks.com Books present the information you need to learn about your report subject. In addition, they show you where to go on the Internet for more information. The pre-evaluated Report Links that back up this book are kept up to date on **www.myreportlinks.com**. With the purchase of a MyReportLinks.com Books title, you and your library gain access to the Report Links that specifically back up that book. The Report Links save hours of research time and link to dozens—even hundreds—of Web sites, source documents, and photos related to your report topic.

Please see "To Our Readers" on the Copyright page for important information about this book, the MyReportLinks.com Books Web site, and the Report Links that back up this book.

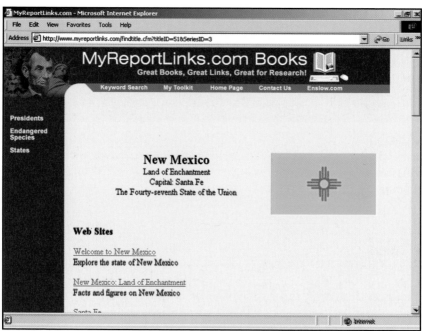

Access:

The Publisher will provide access to the Report Links that back up this book and will try to keep these Report Links up to date on our Web site for three years from the book's first publication date. Please enter **SNM4067** if asked for a password.

Report Links

 The Internet sites described below can be accessed at
http://www.myreportlinks.com

*EDITOR'S CHOICE

▶Welcome to New Mexico
At this Web site you will find information about New Mexico's
government, tourism, agriculture, monuments, and state and
national parks.

Link to this Internet site from http://www.myreportlinks.com

*EDITOR'S CHOICE

▶New Mexico: Land of Enchantment
This site provides facts and figures on the state of New Mexico. Here
you will find the state flag, state symbol, a list of famous New
Mexicans, and other facts and statistical information.

Link to this Internet site from http://www.myreportlinks.com

*EDITOR'S CHOICE

▶Santa Fe
This Web site on Santa Fe is a great tool for planning a visit. Here you
will find places to go, activities, restaurants, and accommodations.
You will also find historical information about Santa Fe.

Link to this Internet site from http://www.myreportlinks.com

*EDITOR'S CHOICE

▶New Mexico
Places to visit, maps, and information on cultural and recreational
activities are included. There is also a travel planner and an interactive
photo tour and video theater.

Link to this Internet site from http://www.myreportlinks.com

*EDITOR'S CHOICE

▶New Mexico
America's Story from America's Library, a Library of Congress Web site,
contains an overview of New Mexico. Learn about the Pueblo Indians,
traditional dance, and the Ralph Edwards Fiesta. You will also find
links to other stories about New Mexico.

Link to this Internet site from http://www.myreportlinks.com

*EDITOR'S CHOICE

▶New Mexico's Cultural Treasures
At this site you can explore New Mexico's parks and monuments,
history, and culture. There are time lines and other resources.

Link to this Internet site from http://www.myreportlinks.com

 The Internet sites described below can be accessed at
http://www.myreportlinks.com

▶**Albuquerque Biological Park**
At this site you will find information on New Mexico's animal life, as well as quizzes and photos.

Link to this Internet site from http://www.myreportlinks.com

▶**The Anasazi and their Hopi Descendants**
At this site you will learn about the Anasazi American Indians and their Hopi descendants. There is also information on preserving the archaeological site and facts about the tribe.

Link to this Internet site from http://www.myreportlinks.com

▶**Billy the Kid Escaped from Jail, April 30, 1881**
America's Story from America's Library, a Library of Congress Web site, presents an overview of how Billy the Kid escaped from jail. You will also learn about Billy the Kid himself.

Link to this Internet site from http://www.myreportlinks.com

▶**Carlsbad Caverns**
The National Park Service Web site provides a brief overview of Carlsbad Caverns. In addition, you will also find a cultural history of the cave, a historic time line, the legislative history of the cave, and other interesting information.

Link to this Internet site from http://www.myreportlinks.com

▶**Constitution of the State of New Mexico adopted January 21, 1911**
At this site you will be able to read New Mexico's state constitution, which is three times as long as the U.S. Constitution.

Link to this Internet site from http://www.myreportlinks.com

▶**Descendants of Mexican War Veterans**
This site brings the Mexican-American War to life. Here you will find images, maps, documents, and historical information about the war.

Link to this Internet site from http://www.myreportlinks.com

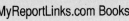
Report Links

The Internet sites described below can be accessed at
http://www.myreportlinks.com

▶ **Don Juan de Oñate**
At this site you will learn interesting facts about Don Juan de Oñate,
the first successful colonizer of the American Southwest. This site also
includes an art gallery.

Link to this Internet site from http://www.myreportlinks.com

▶ **Farmington, New Mexico Convention and Visitors Bureau**
At this site you will find information on the various American
Indian tribes of the Four Corners. Farmington offers outdoor
sports and recreation, and a wonderful array of southwestern
arts and entertainment.

Link to this Internet site from http://www.myreportlinks.com

▶ **Francisco Vázquez de Coronado (1510–1554)**
At this site you will learn the historical importance of Francisco
Vázquez de Coronado, who led one of the most remarkable European
explorations of the North American interior.

Link to this Internet site from http://www.myreportlinks.com

▶ **Georgia O'Keeffe Museum**
At this site you will learn about Georgia O'Keeffe, an artist whose work
was inspired by New Mexico's beautiful landscape.

Link to this Internet site from http://www.myreportlinks.com

▶ **GORP - National Historic Trails - Santa Fe National
Historic Trail**
At this site you will learn about the history of the Santa Fe Trail, which
American and Mexican traders developed as a trade route after Mexico
achieved independence in 1821.

Link to this Internet site from http://www.myreportlinks.com

▶ **Indian Pueblo Cultural Center Hub Page**
At this Web site you can explore the culture, history, and places
occupied by Pueblo Indian tribes, including Acoma Pueblo, Cochiti
Pueblo, Isleta Pueblo, and many others.

Link to this Internet site from http://www.myreportlinks.com

Report Links

 The Internet sites described below can be accessed at
http://www.myreportlinks.com

▶**Manifest Destiny**
This site traces the history of the concept of Manifest Destiny. You will also find essays on Manifest Destiny, which was used to justify the westward expansion of the United States.

Link to this Internet site from http://www.myreportlinks.com

▶**The National Atomic Museum**
At this site you can take a virtual tour and learn the history of the atomic age.

Link to this Internet site from http://www.myreportlinks.com

▶**New Mexico**
The Fact Monster provides you with facts on New Mexico, including famous New Mexicans, government figures, and more.

Link to this Internet site from http://www.myreportlinks.com

▶**New Mexico Magazine Online**
The *New Mexico Magazine* online gives you a sampling of New Mexico's unique culture and the history behind it.

Link to this Internet site from http://www.myreportlinks.com

▶**New Mexico Museum of Natural History and Science**
At this Web site you can explore volcanoes, dinosaurs, fossils, and the natural history of New Mexico.

Link to this Internet site from http://www.myreportlinks.com

▶**New Mexico State Parks**
At this Web site you will find links to the state parks in New Mexico.

Link to this Internet site from http://www.myreportlinks.com

Report Links

The Internet sites described below can be accessed at
http://www.myreportlinks.com

▶ **New Mexico USA: America's Land of Enchantment**
This Web site provides a guide to New Mexico resources on the
Internet. Learn all about New Mexico and its people by playing trivia,
browsing factual tidbits, and exploring New Mexico's people,
businesses, and government.

Link to this Internet site from http://www.myreportlinks.com

▶ **Office of the Governor: New Mexico:**
Governor Gary E. Johnson
At this site you will learn about New Mexico Governor Gary E.
Johnson. You will also find information about the office of the
governor and New Mexico related news.

Link to this Internet site from http://www.myreportlinks.com

▶ **PBS: Weekend Explorer: New Mexico**
PBS features New Mexico in a series called Weekend Explorer. Learn
the history of Billy the Kid, explore the Carlsbad Caverns, or mountain
bike along New Mexico's many scenic trails on your trip.

Link to this Internet site from http://www.myreportlinks.com

▶ **Petroglyph**
The National Park Service Web site provides a brief history of
petroglyphs found in Albuquerque, New Mexico. Here you will learn
about the interesting history of these petroglyphs.

Link to this Internet site from http://www.myreportlinks.com

▶ **Southern New Mexico Online!: The true story of**
Smokey Bear
At this site you will read the history behind the Smokey Bear campaign
and famous slogan.

Link to this Internet site from http://www.myreportlinks.com

▶ **Treaty of Guadalupe Hidalgo**
At this site you will find a brief summary on the Treaty of Guadalupe
Hidalgo, which ended the Mexican-American War. You will also be able
to read the complete treaty.

Link to this Internet site from http://www.myreportlinks.com

Capital
Santa Fe

Population
1,819,046*

Gained Statehood
January 6, 1912

Tree
Pinon, or nut pine

Flower
Yucca

Song
English: "O Fair New Mexico"
Spanish: "Asi es Nuevo Méjico"

Bird
Roadrunner

Insect
Tarantula Hawk Wasp

Fish
Rio Grande Cutthroat Trout

Animal
Black Bear

Gem
Turquoise

Vegetables
Chile and Frijoles (Pinto Beans)

Cookie
Bizcochito

Nickname
"The Land of Enchantment"

Motto
Crescit Eundo (Latin for "It Grows as it Goes.")

Flag
A red Zia Sun symbol on a field of yellow. The colors yellow and red represent the Spanish flag. The Zia Sun in the middle is an ancient sun symbol of the American Indian people known as the Zia. There are four groups of four rays shining from the sun because the Zia believed that the giver of all good gave them gifts in groups of four.[1]

Population reflects the 2000 census.

The State of New Mexico

Three cultures come together in New Mexico: American Indian, Hispanic American, and Anglo American. About 8 percent of New Mexico's population is American Indian.[1]

▶ A State of Many Cultures

Some American Indian tribes, such as the Pueblo, have been there for centuries. The Navajo and Apache came later, but they, too, are long-standing residents. The largest American Indian reservation in the country is the Navajo reservation in the Four Corners area to the northwest. That part of New Mexico is known as Four Corners because the corners of four states—New Mexico, Colorado, Utah, and Arizona—meet there. The reservation lands reach into Arizona and Utah. There are two Apache reservations and nineteen Pueblo reservations in the area. The reservations total nearly 8 million acres of land. The Taos Pueblo, for example, owns 48,000 acres of Blue Lake land, sacred to the tribe.

Today, the Pueblo and Navajo are known for their silver and turquoise jewelry, their thick, hand-woven rugs, and beautiful pottery. The black pottery is especially rare and prized.

The Spanish influence is stronger in New Mexico than in any other state. From the mid-1500s to the mid-to-late-1800s, Spanish culture dominated the area. Today that influence is seen in the area's architecture. Adobe-style houses and churches are reminiscent of Spanish structures. The influence is also evident in the food. The heavy use of

Expresiones Dance Company - Microsoft Internet Explorer

File Edit View Favorites Tools Help

Address [ ] http://www.americaslibrary.gov/pages/es_nm_dance_1_e.html   Go   Links

▲ *The Spanish culture still lingers in New Mexican life today. This photo shows a group of young dancers in traditional dress.*

chili peppers and other spices primarily reflect Mexican tastes. Many places have retained their Spanish names, such as Santa Fe, Cerillos, and Santa Rosa.

By the late 1800s, Anglos, or Americans of non-Hispanic descent, had moved into the territory. Anglos usually, but not always, blended easily with the existing Spanish and American Indian cultures. The early Anglo influence is seen in the red brick houses with tin roofs. Their style is called "territorial" because they were built in the years New Mexico was a United States territory. In the century and a half since the Anglos arrived, the economy and government of New Mexico have followed Anglo models.

Tools   Search   Notes   Discuss   Go!

The Land of Enchantment

New Mexico's nickname is the Land of Enchantment for good reason. It is a land of great beauty, from the towering mountain ranges of central New Mexico to the staked plains (called the *llano estacado*) and dramatic mesas of the eastern part of the state. The high, dry climate of New Mexico creates a deep blue sky that is almost crystal clear. One writer described the state as a land where "sky determines," meaning that the clearness and dryness of the sky seems to be reflected in the entire environment.[2] The magnificent landscape and the rich diversity of cultures attract thousands of tourists annually.

Tourist Attractions

People from around the world come to shop in Santa Fe's expensive jewelry and clothing stores, or to bargain with the American Indians who sell their goods in front of the Governor's Palace on the plaza. Tourists also come to eat in Santa Fe's wide variety of restaurants—ranging from a Chicago-style hot dog stand to pricey cuisine. Once a sleepy town, the state capital of Santa Fe is now a trendy city. Still, it retains the aura of the early days of New Mexico.

Albuquerque, the state's largest city, maintains an area called Old Town, where tourists can shop and dine as though they were in the nineteenth century. Several New Mexico cities have annual outdoor markets featuring either American Indian or Spanish goods. Spanish markets offer religious symbols and paintings, called *santos*, made by artists called *santeros*.

Tourists also visit the pueblos, such as Tesuque Pueblo north of Santa Fe, where many American Indians still live.

▲ *Tourists flock to jewelry stores in New Mexico to buy traditional turquoise and silver jewelry.*

Residents of the Four Corners region also welcome visitors who are willing to drive through the rugged area, but should not expect large settlements or frequent restaurants, gas stations, or even houses. Chaco Canyon in the Four Corners region is one of the most important archeological sites in the country. Here, between 850 A.D. and 1200–1250 A.D., a farming tribe known as the Anasazi created a sophisticated culture. They built a central community, with pueblos three and four stories high, and outlying communities. The Chaco Culture National Historic Park is open to tourists, but there are no accommodations at this remote site.

Carlsbad Caverns National Park in the southern part of the state contains over eighty-five caves, including Lechuguilla Cave, which at 1,567 feet is the country's deepest limestone cave and the third longest. Tours are offered throughout the year.[3]

The Los Alamos National Laboratory opened after World War II, specifically for designing atomic and hydrogen weapons. These weapons were often tested at the White Sands Missile Range in the southern part of the state. Today, the Los Alamos facility does extensive research in energy, environment, and health security. The laboratory is also responsible for the safety and protection of the nation's nuclear weapons stockpile. Parts of the facility are shown to the public on guided tours. Tourists can also visit White Sands National Monument, a beautiful white-sand desert that is ever changing.

Church Influences and the Wild West

For almost three centuries, New Mexico was dominated not only by Spain, but also by the Roman Catholic Church. One of the most interesting and controversial figures in the state's history is French-born Bishop Jean Baptiste Lamy. He came to Santa Fe in 1851 and began building churches and starting educational programs. But he did not get along well with local priests because he removed some priests from their posts whom he thought were corrupt.[4] He became the subject of a classic novel by Willa Cather, *Death Comes for the Archbishop*.

New Mexico was also part of the Wild West fame. William Bonney, better known as Billy the Kid, killed seventeen men before he died at the age of twenty-one.[5] The Kid did most of his killing during the infamous Lincoln County War, which was over rustling (stealing

▲ *The Roman Catholic Church had a major impact on New Mexican culture and society. The architecture of this church shows a blend of traditional church and adobe styles.*

livestock) in southern New Mexico.[6] There is a historical marker at the spot in southern New Mexico near Fort Sumner where lawman Pat Garrett trapped and killed the Kid. Kit Carson was another legendary Old West figure from New Mexico. He was a guide and eventually a general in the U. S. Army.

▶ New Mexico's Authors

New Mexico claims many well-known authors. Perhaps the earliest was Governor Lew Wallace, who in 1880 completed *Ben Hur*, a historical novel which tells of the rise of Christianity in the Roman Empire. Best known today is mystery writer Tony Hillerman, who has created a fictional police team of Joe Leaphorn and Jim Chee. The older, retired Leaphorn and the younger Chee are members of the Navajo tribal police force on the Four Corners reservation.

One of the leading Hispanic-American writers today is Rudolfo Anaya. His best-known work is *Bless Me, Ultima,* a novel about a young Chicano boy in the plains of southeastern New Mexico in the 1940s. The "Ultima" of the title is the boy's grandmother, a traditional *curandero,* or spiritual healer.

John Nichols of Taos is best known for his novel, *The Milagro Beanfield War.* The novel tells of the small farmers and shepherds of the dirt-poor town of Milagro who fight developers who want to steal their land. One man's bean field becomes the symbol of the poor men's struggle. The novel was later made into a popular movie.

The late Paul Horgan wrote primarily nonfiction about New Mexico, including a two-volume history of the Rio Grande, a book about artist Henriette Wyeth Hurd, and an account of the life of Bishop Lamy.

Artists

New Mexico's dramatic landscapes have attracted a number of artists. Georgia O'Keeffe lived most of her life in New York City but is forever associated with New Mexico. She created dramatic large-scale paintings of flowers and stark, abstract paintings of the state's mountains, the sun-bleached bones and exotic flowers found in desert areas, and the adobe churches. For some years, she worked at Ghost Ranch in Abiquiu near Taos.

Henriette Wyeth Hurd was the daughter of famed East Coast illustrator N. C. Wyeth and the sister of watercolorist Andrew Wyeth. She married New Mexican artist Peter Hurd. They established a western branch of this

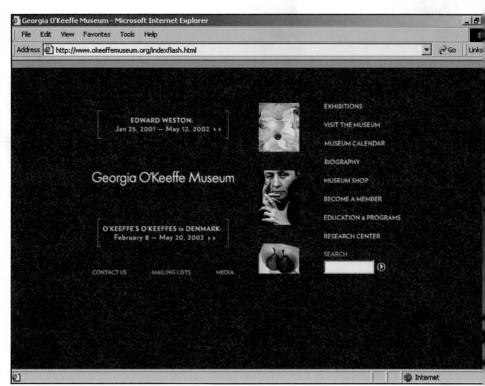

Georgia O'Keeffe Museum - Microsoft Internet Explorer

File   Edit   View   Favorites   Tools   Help

Address http://www.okeeffemuseum.org/indexflash.html   Go   Links

EDWARD WESTON:
Jan 25, 2001 — May 12, 2002

Georgia O'Keeffe Museum

O'KEEFFE'S O'KEEFFES in DENMARK:
February 8 — May 20, 2002

CONTACT US   MAILING LISTS   MEDIA

EXHIBITIONS

VISIT THE MUSEUM

MUSEUM CALENDAR

BIOGRAPHY

MUSEUM SHOP

BECOME A MEMBER

EDUCATION & PROGRAMS

RESEARCH CENTER

SEARCH

Internet

▲ *New Mexico's breathtaking landscapes captured the attention of artist Georgia O'Keeffe.*

distinguished artistic family at San Patricio. Peter Hurd painted primarily landscapes of the land he lived on and loved. Henriette Wyeth Hurd created portraits and still life works. Some of their children and at least one grandchild are working artists today, as are many members of the eastern branch of the family. The Wyeth Hurd Gallery in Santa Fe displays the family's work.

The potter known simply as María is legendary as the master of the Navajo potters. She lived in the San Ildefonso Pueblo and began making pots at the age of ten. She marked her pots by putting her handprint inside them. Sometimes she signed her name to the best pots made by other women so that they could ask a better price. Legend says that she and her husband, Julian, made the first black pot by mistake. They were firing pots, but the fire went out and smoke colored the clay. Today María's black pots are high-priced collector's items. María, who lived into her nineties, was invited to the White House by five presidents and was awarded a grant by the important National Endowment for the Arts.

American Indian artist R. C. Gorman enjoyed a great burst of popularity in the 1980s with his portraits of stylized American Indian women. At the start of the twenty-first century he maintained galleries in Taos and Santa Fe.

▲ This photo shows a few of famous potter María's creations. Many of these black pots are collector's items and cost thousands of dollars.

Chapter 2

Landscape and Climate

New Mexico is the fifth largest state in the nation, with 78 million acres of land. Much of this land is owned either by the state or the federal government. According to the 2000 U.S. Census, the state has a population of 1,819,046, making it the thirty-sixth state in population.

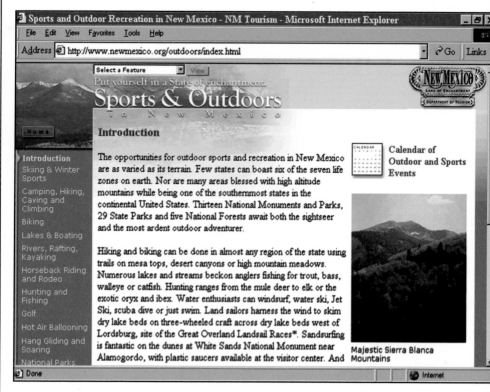

Sports and Outdoor Recreation in New Mexico - NM Tourism - Microsoft Internet Explorer

File　Edit　View　Favorites　Tools　Help

Address http://www.newmexico.org/outdoors/index.html ▾ 𝒫Go　Links

Select a Feature ▾ View

Put yourself in a State of enchantment.

Sports & Outdoors
In New Mexico

NEW MEXICO
LAND OF ENCHANTMENT
DEPARTMENT OF TOURISM

Home

Introduction

Introduction
Skiing & Winter Sports
Camping, Hiking, Caving and Climbing
Biking
Lakes & Boating
Rivers, Rafting, Kayaking
Horseback Riding and Rodeo
Hunting and Fishing
Golf
Hot Air Ballooning
Hang Gliding and Soaring
National Parks

Calendar of Outdoor and Sports Events

The opportunities for outdoor sports and recreation in New Mexico are as varied as its terrain. Few states can boast six of the seven life zones on earth. Nor are many areas blessed with high altitude mountains while being one of the southernmost states in the continental United States. Thirteen National Monuments and Parks, 29 State Parks and five National Forests await both the sightseer and the most ardent outdoor adventurer.

Hiking and biking can be done in almost any region of the state using trails on mesa tops, desert canyons or high mountain meadows. Numerous lakes and streams beckon anglers fishing for trout, bass, walleye or catfish. Hunting ranges from the mule deer to elk or the exotic oryx and ibex. Water enthusiasts can windsurf, water ski, Jet Ski, scuba dive or just swim. Land sailors harness the wind to skim dry lake beds on three-wheeled craft across dry lake beds west of Lordsburg, site of the Great Overland Landsail Races*. Sandsurfing is fantastic on the dunes at White Sands National Monument near Alamogordo, with plastic saucers available at the visitor center. And

Majestic Sierra Blanca Mountains

Done Internet

▲ The Sierra Blanca mountain range is located in the southern part of the Rocky Mountains.

Tools   Search   Notes   Discuss   Go!

▲ *The eastern part of New Mexico consists mainly of plains, with grassland and sagebrush.*

Between 1990 and 2000, the population increased twenty percent, suggesting that New Mexico is attracting new residents at a fairly high rate. New Mexicans are highly concentrated in a few areas. One-third of the people live in Bernalillo County, which includes the city of Albuquerque.[1] In contrast, large parts of the New Mexico landscape are without residents.

▶ A State of Many Landscapes

The landscape ranges from red canyon land in the northwest to pine-forest mountains over 13,000 feet high in the north-central part of the state. The Great Plains extend westward from Texas into the eastern part of the state. The plains, with grassland and sagebrush, gradually descend as they roll south. In the southeast corner of the

state the land is at sea level. Not much grows in the south and southwestern parts of the state where this land of rolling hills is about 3,000 to 4,000 feet above sea level. There are lava beds and blocks of black rock called malpais, which are treacherous to both people and horses. In other parts of the south and southwest there are long stretches of flat, brown land.[2]

▶ Climate

New Mexico is a dry state, with an average rainfall of only about ten inches a year. Only 0.2 percent of its land surface is water, the smallest percentage of any state in the nation. The state's major rivers—the Rio Grande, San Juan, Chama, and Pecos—could be considered streams in

▲ *Beautiful skies and scenery are common sights in New Mexico.*

another location and climate. A great deal of moisture, in the form of snow, falls in the mountains. Some mountains near Taos and Santa Fe can get as much as three hundred inches of snow in a year. Much of New Mexico relies on spring runoff of melting snow in the mountains for its water supply.[3] Because the air is extremely dry, raindrops sometimes evaporate before reaching the ground. This is called a dry rain.

The high, dry climate creates the fresh air and the clear, blue skies for which New Mexico is famous. Before it was called the Land of Enchantment, New Mexico called itself the Sunshine State because the sun shines about seventy percent of the time. In the summer months, thunderstorms often build up in the mountains in the late afternoons, occasionally putting clouds in the sky.[4]

Flash floods are the most common natural disaster. When rain does come, it is often fast and heavy. Since the hard, dry soil cannot absorb the water, there is no place for it to go except downhill. When there is a flash flood the weather may be sunny and clear, but water comes from rain in the mountains. This rapid runoff gathers strength and speed in low-lying dry gulches or ditches called arroyos. Flash floods can wash away cars or people in an instant. In recent years, strategically placed concrete arroyos have been built to control runoff and avoid flash floods.

Dust storms are another problem. When rain has been particularly scarce, the dry earth is blown about by the strong western winds. These storms create a breathing problem for many people.

Economy

Historically, New Mexico has been considered a poor state. It has a large number of wealthy citizens, who live in such places as Santa Fe and Riudoso, where there is a famous horse-racing track. Still, New Mexico has a much larger number of people living at or below the poverty level. In 1990, it was the third poorest state in the

Taos Pueblo, New Mexico - Microsoft Internet Explorer

File   Edit   View   Favorites   Tools   Help

Address http://www.americaslibrary.gov/pages/es_nm_pueblo_1_e.html   Go   Links

Taos Pueblo, New Mexico   ◀BACK

Taos Pueblo, New Mexico

Internet

▲ The American Indian population of New Mexico lived in poverty for many years. This is a photo of the Taos Pueblo during the Great Depression.

country.[1] In 1991, the state's citizens ranked forty-sixth in income per person.[2] For many years, the American Indian population lived in extreme poverty. Their lifestyle has improved in recent years, but there is room for more improvement. American Indians receive more financial aid from the federal government than the general population.

▶ Income

The state has traditionally had three sources of income—tourism, federal spending, and natural resources. Tourists visit the state's many historic sites, especially those related to the Hispanic and American Indian cultures. There are major ski resorts at Taos, Santa Fe, Ruidoso, and Angel Fire. Although Hispanic Americans and American Indians were initially hesitant about sharing their culture with outsiders, they seem to have somewhat embraced tourism as a source of income. The Mescalero Apache tribe has opened the Sierra Blanca ski resort in the Sacramento Mountains near Alamogordo, and the Jicarilla Apache operate a lodge at Stone Lake in the Four Corners. American Indian tribes also operate gambling casinos.

National parks include Bandolier National Monument, White Sands National Monument, and the Carlsbad Caverns. Many of these scenic landmarks draw film and television production companies to the state.

Federal spending supports two national research laboratories and several defense installations, as well as extensive social service programs. Federal dollars provide health care and education services, from free lunch programs to college loans. Federal funds support irrigation and farm programs, and highway development as well. The state has an unusually high number of citizens employed by federal, state, and local governments.

▶ Mineral Resources and the Environment

Mineral resources have declined in importance to New Mexico's economy. During the extensive atomic testing after World War II, there was great demand for previously useless uranium deposits. At the same time, national and international markets for copper, potash, and coal began to decline gradually. In addition, the challenge of saving the environment affected recovery of mineral resources. Petroleum producers, who once saw their business decline, have found new markets in cities on the West Coast. Most of the petroleum is produced in the Four Corners area.[3]

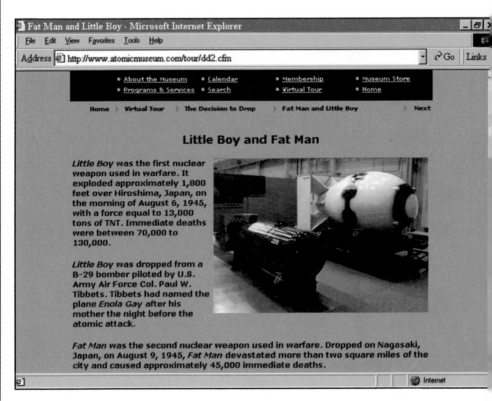

▲ Little Boy and Fat Man, the first nuclear weapons ever to be used in warfare, were constructed in New Mexico.

Although mineral resources are no longer as important as they once were, manufacturing has increased. Principal products are electronic and biomedical equipment, and highways and railroad equipment. U.S. Census Bureau figures for 1997 indicate manufacturing had the highest sales in the state, followed by retail trade. Retail trade is high because of tourism.[4]

New Mexico's long years of poverty are closely linked to the state's isolation. As a Mexican province, it was far from its government. That situation did not improve with territorial status and statehood. During the last half of the twentieth century, however, technological changes from airplanes, to television, to the Internet, linked the state to the rest of the country.

Government

The New Mexican government has remained basically unchanged for the last fifty years. The state has operated under the same constitution since 1910. The state constitution was submitted by a special convention when they were applying for statehood. It is three times as long as the U.S. Constitution, and is difficult to amend or change.[1] In 1992, Governor Bruce King was unsuccessful when he called for major revisions of what he called an "antiquated document."[2]

▶ The Executive Branch

Various reforms in the late twentieth century attempted to centralize governmental powers. For example, the governor is now elected for a four-year term and can run for re-election only once.[3]

As the highest elected official, the governor is responsible for the day-to-day operations of the state and for its financial affairs. He also has a strong veto power over legislation presented to him, and can pardon certain convicted criminals. Yet his power can be limited by other elected officials and numerous boards, agencies, and commissions, which also have a great deal of authority.

The lieutenant governor is also elected. He presides over the legislature and breaks tie votes. He is not a major political figure in the state. Other elected officials are the secretary of state, auditor, commissioner of public lands, treasurer, and attorney general (who must be a lawyer).

Tools   Search   Notes   Discuss   Go!

Some boards and commissions are elected, such as the three-member Corporation Commission. The governor also appoints some, such as members of the State Highway Commission. The Board of Education has fifteen members—ten are elected and the governor appoints five.[4] By 1969, the number of agencies had grown out of hand—as many as two hundred agencies were combined into twelve major cabinet departments.[5] Today agencies are periodically discontinued unless they can convince the legislature that they are needed.[6]

▶ An Old Way of Governing

Many units of government do not reflect the state's shift in the last half of the twentieth century from a rural to an

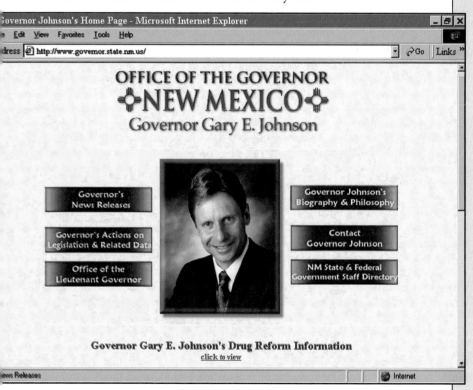

▲ Governor Gary E. Johnson was first elected in 1994.

urban state. For instance, there are numerous school districts, because voters resist efforts to consolidate several districts into one. Similarly, there are many local governments with little coordination between them.

New Mexico's legislature meets at noon on the third Tuesday of January every year in Santa Fe. In odd-numbered years, the forty-two senators and seventy members of the House of Representatives meet for a "long session" of sixty days. In even-numbered years, they have a "short session" of thirty days.[7] The governor can call a special session. Interim committees meet between sessions. Attempts to lengthen the sessions have repeatedly failed.

In New Mexico, every effort is made to balance the legislature ethnically between Anglos and Hispanics, although women are still underrepresented. At the beginning of the twenty-first century, several American Indians were also serving in the legislature.

Members of the legislature are not paid a salary but are given a per diem, or daily fee. As a result, members do not represent economic diversity. Blue collar and agricultural workers cannot afford to be legislators. Attempts to introduce a salary system have been resisted.

Judges are recommended by a committee, appointed by the governor, and then finally elected. They run as representatives of either the Republican or Democratic parties. The party system is strong in the state, and there is a high voter turnout in elections. New Mexico has been a Democratic state since the 1930s, especially in its rural and Hispanic-American communities. In recent years there has been a shift to the Republican Party. The Democratic Party has managed to retain a majority, but the 2000 presidential election was close between the two parties.[8]

Nations Within a Nation

New Mexico has some special circumstances because of its large American Indian population. Federal law considers American Indian reservations dependent nations—or separate nations within a nation. The state has little power over the reservations. Tribes elect officers, usually a president, vice president, and tribal council. These officers settle most matters. The federal government handles problems over which the tribe does not have authority, such as major crimes. The United States government, not the state, has supreme power over reservation matters. Yet

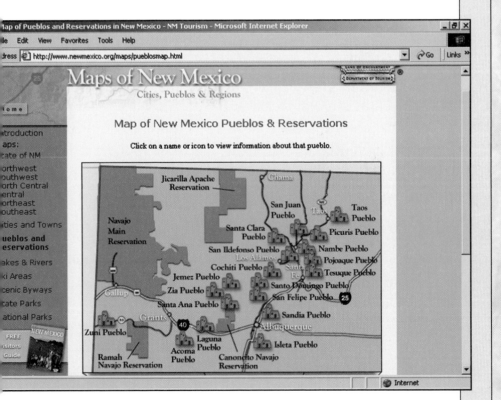

▲ This map shows the American Indian reservations in New Mexico.

residents of the reservation vote in local, state, and federal elections and hold elected offices at local and state levels.

The state cannot tax money earned on reservation land. That right belongs to the tribe. The tribes control their land, water, and other natural resources. For instance, fishing on reservation lands requires a tribal license, not a state license. Tribes can also regulate the sale of liquor on their lands. In effect, the New Mexican state government has no control over large portions of the territory within its boundaries.

History

New Mexico has some of the oldest continuously inhabited settlements in North America. American Indians have occupied the same villages and pueblos for hundreds of years. Unlike the Plains Indians, they were never driven from their homes by the influx of Anglos. Santa Fe, established by the Spaniards, was inhabited before the Pilgrims arrived at Plymouth Rock in 1620. Some New Mexicans of Spanish and Mexican ancestry can trace their origins to the sixteenth century.

The state's history is generally considered to fall into six periods: prehistory, the era of Spanish exploration, the Spanish colonial period, the Mexican years, the territorial years, and statehood.

▶ Prehistory

Archeological evidence suggests people lived on the land as much as thirty thousand years ago. Bones and artifacts found at a site near Clovis documents human residents over thirteen thousand years ago. The Anasazi, who lived in the northwest portion of the state, were at first hunters who followed game animals from place to place. By about 3000 B.C., they began to roam less and gathered wild foods instead. Because they now stayed in one place, they had more time to weave baskets, make pottery, and develop their architecture. Their villages were built around a cen-tral plaza with a circular ceremonial chamber. Pueblo Bonito at Chaco Canyon is the largest such ruin in North

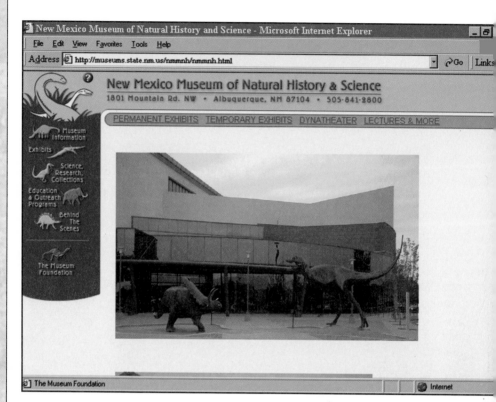

New Mexico Museum of Natural History and Science - Microsoft Internet Explorer

File Edit View Favorites Tools Help

Address http://museums.state.nm.us/nmmnh/nmmnh.html   Go   Links

New Mexico Museum of Natural History & Science
1801 Mountain Rd. NW • Albuquerque, NM 87104 • 505-841-2800

PERMANENT EXHIBITS TEMPORARY EXHIBITS DYNATHEATER LECTURES & MORE

Museum Information
Exhibits
Science, Research, Collections
Education & Outreach Programs
Behind The Scenes
The Museum Foundation

The Museum Foundation   Internet

▲ These two life-size bronze statues of New Mexico dinosaurs give a glimpse into New Mexico's prehistoric period.

America. It illustrates the complexity of the Anasazi stone and cliff dwellings.[1]

In the southwestern portion of the state, American Indians of the Mogollon culture were closer to Mexico and therefore developed villages and communities before the Anasazi. But the Anasazi surpassed them with more sophisticated architecture and community life. Today the Mogollon culture is studied only by scholars. The influence of the Anasazi is much stronger, for they are the ancestors of today's Pueblo Indians.[2]

Droughts periodically forced these natives to move away from their villages. The worst drought occurred in 1300 A.D. Most existing pueblos date from the late 1500s.[3]

The Era of Spanish Exploration

Spanish exploration began in the mid-sixteenth century. Conquistador Francisco Coronado was the first Spaniard to lead an expedition across the state. He was searching for the Seven Cities of Cibola believed to hold enormous treasure. Instead of gold, he found turquoise, which he did not think was valuable. Although the inhabitants of the

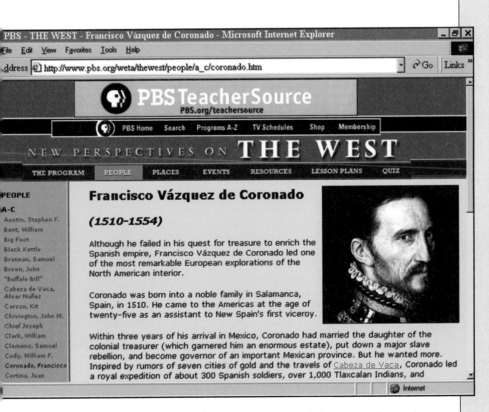

PBS - THE WEST - Francisco Vázquez de Coronado - Microsoft Internet Explorer

File   Edit   View   Favorites   Tools   Help

Address http://www.pbs.org/weta/thewest/people/a_c/coronado.htm   Go   Links

PBS TeacherSource
PBS.org/teachersource

PBS Home   Search   Programs A-Z   TV Schedules   Shop   Membership

NEW PERSPECTIVES ON **THE WEST**

THE PROGRAM   PEOPLE   PLACES   EVENTS   RESOURCES   LESSON PLANS   QUIZ

PEOPLE
A-C
Austin, Stephen F.
Bent, William
Big Foot
Black Kettle
Brannan, Samuel
Brown, John
"Buffalo Bill"
Cabeza de Vaca, Alvar Nuñez
Carson, Kit
Chivington, John M.
Chief Joseph
Clark, William
Clemens, Samuel
Cody, William F.
Coronado, Francisco
Cortina, Juan

Francisco Vázquez de Coronado

(1510-1554)

Although he failed in his quest for treasure to enrich the Spanish empire, Francisco Vázquez de Coronado led one of the most remarkable European explorations of the North American interior.

Coronado was born into a noble family in Salamanca, Spain, in 1510. He came to the Americas at the age of twenty-five as an assistant to New Spain's first viceroy.

Within three years of his arrival in Mexico, Coronado had married the daughter of the colonial treasurer (which garnered him an enormous estate), put down a major slave rebellion, and become governor of an important Mexican province. But he wanted more. Inspired by rumors of seven cities of gold and the travels of Cabeza de Vaca, Coronado led a royal expedition of about 300 Spanish soldiers, over 1,000 Tlaxcalan Indians, and

Internet

▲ Francisco Vázquez de Coronado led one of the most thorough European expeditions of the North American interior.

pueblos welcomed Coronado, he abused their hospitality and eventually killed many of them.

The Spanish Colonial Period

Two hundred eighty-one years of Spanish rule followed. Colonists under Governor Don Juan de Oñate established the first successful settlement in 1598. Santa Fe was established in 1609.[4] During the colonial years, natives and Spaniards mostly raised livestock and farmed. There was some mining, but it disappointed the Spanish because they found no precious minerals. In addition to gold, the Spanish explorers looked for the Northwest Passage. They

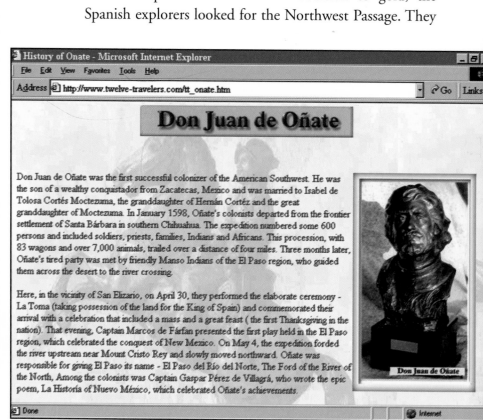

History of Onate - Microsoft Internet Explorer

File Edit View Favorites Tools Help

Address http://www.twelve-travelers.com/tt_onate.htm　Go Links

Don Juan de Oñate

Don Juan de Oñate was the first successful colonizer of the American Southwest. He was the son of a wealthy conquistador from Zacatecas, Mexico and was married to Isabel de Tolosa Cortés Moctezuma, the granddaughter of Hernán Cortéz and the great granddaughter of Moctezuma. In January 1598, Oñate's colonists departed from the frontier settlement of Santa Bárbara in southern Chihuahua. The expedition numbered some 600 persons and included soldiers, priests, families, Indians and Africans. This procession, with 83 wagons and over 7,000 animals, trailed over a distance of four miles. Three months later, Oñate's tired party was met by friendly Manso Indians of the El Paso region, who guided them across the desert to the river crossing.

Here, in the vicinity of San Elizario, on April 30, they performed the elaborate ceremony - La Toma (taking possession of the land for the King of Spain) and commemorated their arrival with a celebration that included a mass and a great feast (the first Thanksgiving in the nation). That evening, Captain Marcos de Fárfan presented the first play held in the El Paso region, which celebrated the conquest of New Mexico. On May 4, the expedition forded the river upstream near Mount Cristo Rey and slowly moved northward. Oñate was responsible for giving El Paso its name - El Paso del Río del Norte, The Ford of the River of the North. Among the colonists was Captain Gaspar Pérez de Villagrá, who wrote the epic poem, La Historía of Nuevo México, which celebrated Oñate's achievements.

Don Juan de Oñate

Done　Internet

Don Juan de Oñate was the first successful colonizer of the American Southwest.

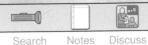
believed it was a water route between the Atlantic and Pacific oceans.

The Spanish also came to convert the native population to Christianity. The Pueblo Indians were settled in one place, and as a result, were easier to convert than the warlike and nomadic Navajo and Apache tribes. The Spanish strongly encouraged the natives to convert to Catholicism, and many accepted the new religion or parts of it. Even today many American Indians practice a religion that blends native religions with Christianity. Since the Spanish brought no women with them, the colonial period witnessed a great deal of intermarriage between the natives and the Spanish.

In 1680, the Pueblo Indians revolted against the Spanish. It was the most successful revolution by a native population against a European one in North American history. As a result, the Spanish were kept out of the region for thirteen years.

Spain would not allow its provinces to trade with other countries. Periodically, French traders approached New Mexico. Spain sent expeditions against them, but with little success. In 1763, the French and Indian War ended France's control over large portions of North America. Later, Spain also forbade trade with the United States. In 1807, American Lieutenant Zebulon M. Pike led an expedition into the Spanish southwest to explore the area for the United States government. He was arrested by the Spanish and taken to Santa Fe, but was later released.

▶ Under Mexican Rule

In 1821, Mexico gained its independence from Spain and New Mexico became a Mexican province. Mexico allowed trade with other countries. William Becknell rode from

Franklin, Missouri, to Santa Fe, bringing goods to trade. Becknell had items Santa Fe residents could not get from Mexico, and he returned to Missouri a rich man. He is credited with opening the Santa Fe Trail between Independence, Missouri, and New Mexico's capital city. There had long been a Santa Fe Trail to Mexico City, but

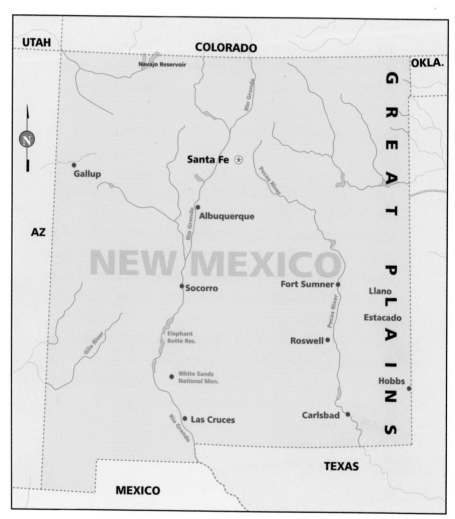

▲ The state of New Mexico.

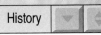

it was difficult to bring supplies over that long road. Becknell's trail changed life in New Mexico dramatically.

Anglo adventurers on the Santa Fe Trail encountered dangers and difficulties, such as American Indian attacks and high tariffs from the Mexican government. In the early 1830s, fur traders Charles Bent and Ceran St. Vrain formed a partnership to establish a permanent trading base in Santa Fe. Later, Bent built the largest trading post in the United States on the Santa Fe Trail, southeast of present-day Colorado Springs, Colorado.

The Territorial Years

In the United States, there was growing interest in the concept of Manifest Destiny. The United States government believed it was destined to control the land from the Atlantic to Pacific oceans. Americans began to move to, and establish businesses in New Mexico, mostly in Santa Fe. In 1841, an expedition of three hundred men and fourteen wagons marched from Texas to New Mexico. Texas claimed all land east of the Rio Grande. This claim would have given the Texans much of New Mexico's land, and established trade routes for Texas. The Mexican government captured the expedition.

By 1846, the United Sates was at war with Mexico over the question of boundaries. The border between Texas and Mexico was the focus of the conflict, but New Mexico was included. Santa Fe was occupied by American troops under General Stephen Watts Kearny. When Kearny believed the city safe, he withdrew and appointed Charles Bent governor. Bent was assassinated by Mexicans and American Indians at his home in Taos, north of Santa Fe. The Mexican-American War ended with the 1848 Treaty of Guadalupe Hidalgo, which gave the United States

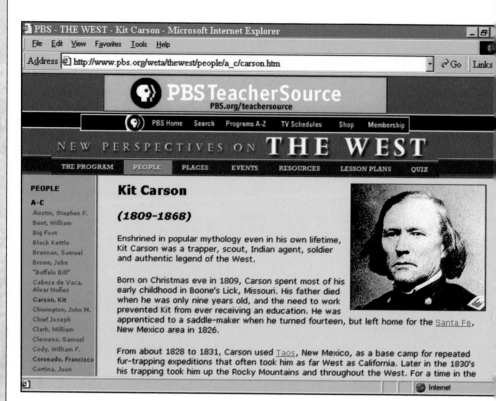

▲ Kit Carson was a famous frontiersman who helped guide John C. Fremont's second expedition, which included a survey of Great Salt Lake in Utah and part of the Oregon Trail.

much of what is now the southwestern part of the country, including New Mexico. This ended the Spanish colonial period and in the period of New Mexico's status as a territory of the United States.

▶ Statehood

New Mexico entered the Union as a territory because its population was primarily Catholic and Spanish-speaking.[5] Members of the U.S. Congress objected to that for sixty-two years. In addition, Congress at that time was bitterly divided between representatives of free states and slave states. New Mexico would have entered as a free state, but senators and legislators from slave states successfully opposed statehood for New Mexico.

Early in the Civil War, Texas, a Confederate state, sent an expedition to force New Mexico to join the Confederacy. The Texans were defeated in the Battle of Glorieta Pass, the only Civil War battle fought on New Mexican ground. The territory remained in the Union.

▶ The Last of the American Indian Raids

Navajo, Apache, Comanche, and Ute Indians had raided both Spanish settlements and the peaceful Pueblo Indians for years. A major defeat of these tribes in the late 1700s opened the way for more Spanish settlement of the area, yet the problem continued. During the Civil War, American soldier Kit Carson was ordered to round up the Mescalero Apache and Navajo tribes and forced them onto reservations to learn Anglo ways. In 1886, the United States government finally defeated the legendary Geronimo and his Chiricahua Apache, thus bringing an end to the American Indian raids in New Mexico.

▶ Railroads

The arrival of the Atchison, Topeka and Santa Fe Railroad early in the twentieth century brought Anglo culture to New Mexico. Tourism began, and American Indian bowls and rugs became souvenirs instead of useful items of daily life. This popularity encouraged a romanticizing of the past—the revival, for instance of the flat-roofed adobe buildings of Pueblo architecture. In the twenty-first century, tourists still buy bowls, rugs, jewelry, blankets, and other Southwestern items.

Billy the Kid Escaped from Jail - Microsoft Internet Explorer

File Edit View Favorites Tools Help

Address http://www.americaslibrary.gov/pages/jb_0430_billykid_1_e.html Go Links

Done Internet

▲ *Billy the Kid escaped from a jail cell similar to this one.*

The railroad also created a problem. Because ranchers could ship beef east, cattle raising became very profitable. Range wars broke out between large ranch owners and small ranchers, who accused one another of rustling. The most famous range war was the Lincoln County War that occurred in the late 1870s. Small ranchers opposed big landowners John Henry Tunstall and Alexander McSween. Billy the Kid sided with Tunstall and McSween. When Tunstall was killed, the war became one of revenge. The small ranchers held McSween's forces under siege in his ranch house. Susan McSween played battle songs on the piano to encourage the men. Then the piano was shot to pieces and the house burned. McSween was killed, but Billy the Kid escaped.[6]

▶ Recent Problems

The first part of the twentieth century was unremarkable for New Mexico. It remained a poor state. Like other southwestern states, it suffered through the Great Depression and the Dust Bowl during the 1930s. The Dust Bowl was an ecological disaster caused by drought and bad farming practices. Strong winds blew soil into the air, ruining farmlands and causing people to have to leave their homes. When federal aid programs were introduced, New Mexico received a large share of the available money.

The onset of World War II transformed the state. People moved to the cities. Both the Hispanic-American and American Indian cultures supported the war effort, and some joined the Armed Forces. Others went to work in war-related industries, particularly on the West Coast. Many never returned to the communities of their childhood. The establishment of military sites created new job opportunities for residents who had remained. The federal government built Kirtland Air Force Base near Albuquerque, Cannon Air Force Base near Clovis, Walker Air Force Base for atomic testing near Roswell, and Holloman Air Force Base at the White Sands Missile Range. Many New Mexicans worked at these bases and lived in the nearby cities.

▶ New Transformations

World War II also converted the state into a scientific community. Before 1940, there were few scientific institutions. The Manhattan Project, which developed the first atomic bomb, brought leading physicists such as Robert

Oppenheimer and Enrico Fermi to New Mexico. The federal government established the laboratories at Los Alamos. The first atomic bomb was exploded near Alamogordo on July 16, 1945.

After World War II, the Cold War, a standoff between the Soviet Union and the United States, led the U.S. Congress to support weapons research with heavy funding. This money bolstered the economy of New Mexico. Scientists came from all parts of the country to live in New Mexico.

In the last half of the twentieth century, New Mexico grew in ways similar to many other western states. Tourism continues to increase, but the population also grows at a fast rate as people leave the crowded east and west coasts for more open lands. These newcomers tend to cluster in cities and the small towns near them. Manufacturing and education have also developed, increasing the economic base.

Surprisingly, New Mexico, once a rural state at the outset of World War II, is now a thoroughly urban state. Albuquerque has an international airport; most cities have all the same fast-food restaurants and chain motels that are found across the country. The hope is that New Mexico will be able to retain its unique blend of cultures and its strong sense of history in the face of rapid growth and technological change.

Chapter Notes

New Mexico Facts

1. *USA State Symbols,* Flags & Facts, CD-ROM, Canada: Robesus, Inc., 2001.

Chapter 1. The State of New Mexico

1. Paul L. Hain, F. Chris Garcia, and Gilbert K. St. Clair, eds., *New Mexico Government,* Third ed. (Albuquerque: University of New Mexico Press, 1994), p. 193.

2. Ross Calvin, *Sky Determines* (Albuquerque: University of New Mexico Press, 1965).

3. Carlsbad Caverns, *National Park Service,* n.d., <http://www.nps.gov/cave/> (May 18, 2001).

4. Thomas E. Chávez, *An Illustrated History of New Mexico* (Niwot: University Press of Colorado, 1992), p. 12.

5. Paul Trachtman, *The Old West: The Gunfighters* (New York: Time-Life Books, 1974), p. 168.

6. Ibid., pp. 183–190.

Chapter 2. Landscape and Climate

1. Paul L. Hain, F. Chris Garcia, and Gilbert K. St. Clair, eds., *New Mexico Government,* Third ed. (Albuquerque: University of New Mexico Press, 1994), pp. 1–2.

2. Marc Simmons, *New Mexico: A Bicentennial History* (New York: W. W. Norton & Company, Inc. 1977), p. 191.

3. Hain et. al, p. 2.

4. "New Mexico's Climate: Mild and Sunny Year Round," *New Mexico Travel Planner,* n.d., <http://www.newmexico.org/visitor/climate.html> (January 29, 2002).

Chapter 3. Economy

1. Paul L. Hain, F. Chris Garcia, and Gilbert K. St. Clair, eds., *New Mexico Government,* Third ed. (Albuquerque: University of New Mexico Press, 1994), p. 6.

2. Richard W. Etulain, ed., *Contemporary New Mexico, 1940–1990* (Albuquerque: University of New Mexico Press, 1994), p. 63.

3. Ibid., p. 18.

4. Ibid.

Chapter 4. Government

1. Richard W. Etulain, ed., *Contemporary New Mexico, 1940–1990* (Albuquerque: University of New Mexico Press, 1994), p. 33.

2. Ibid., p. 29.

3. Paul L. Hain, F. Chris Garcia, and Gilbert K. St. Clair, eds., *New Mexico Government*, Third ed. (Albuquerque: University of New Mexico Press, 1994), p. 20.

4. Ibid., p. 19.

5. Etulain, p. 46.

6. Hain et. al, p. 299.

7. Ibid., p. 35.

8. Etulain, pp. 51–53.

Chapter 5. History

1. Thomas E. Chávez, *An Illustrated History of New Mexico* (Niwot: University Press of Colorado, 1992), p. 3.

2. Ibid., p. 2.

3. Ibid., p. 4.

4. Ibid., p. 6.

5. Robert J. Torrez, "The Quest for Statehood," *New Mexico—A* History, 1991, <http://www.sos.state.nm.us /BLUEBOOK/hist07.htm> (February 1, 2002).

6. Ross Calvin, *Sky Determines* (Albuquerque: University of New Mexico Press, 1965), pp. 269–270.

Further Reading

Alter, Judy. *The Santa Fe Trail.* Danbury, Conn.: Children's Press, 1998.

Baldwin, Louis. *Intruders Within: Pueblo Resistance to Spanish Rule & the Revolt of 1680.* Danbury, Conn.: Watts, Franklin Watts, Inc., 1995.

Calvin, Ross. *Sky Determines: An Interpretation of the Southwest.* Boulder, Colo.: High-Lonesome Books, 1993.

Chávez, Thomas E. *An Illustrated History of New Mexico.* Niwot: University Press of Colorado, 1992.

Dick-Peddie, William A. *New Mexico Vegetation: Past, Present, & Future.* Albuquerque: University of New Mexico Press, 1993.

Etulain, Richard W., ed. *Contemporary New Mexico, 1940–1990.* Albuquerque: University of New Mexico Press, 1994.

Hain, Paul L., F. Chris Garcia, and Gilbert K. St. Clair, eds. *New Mexico Government.* Third ed. Albuquerque: University of New Mexico Press, 1994.

Kavanaugh, James. *New Mexico Wildlife.* Blaine, Wash.: Waterford Press, Ltd., 1998.

Kent, Deborah. *New Mexico.* Second ed. Danbury, Conn.: Children's Press, 1999.

Larson, Carole. *Forgotten Frontier: The Story of Southeastern New Mexico.* Albuquerque: University of New Mexico Press, 1993.

Roberts, Susan A. *History of New Mexico.* Albuquerque: University of New Mexico Press, 1991.